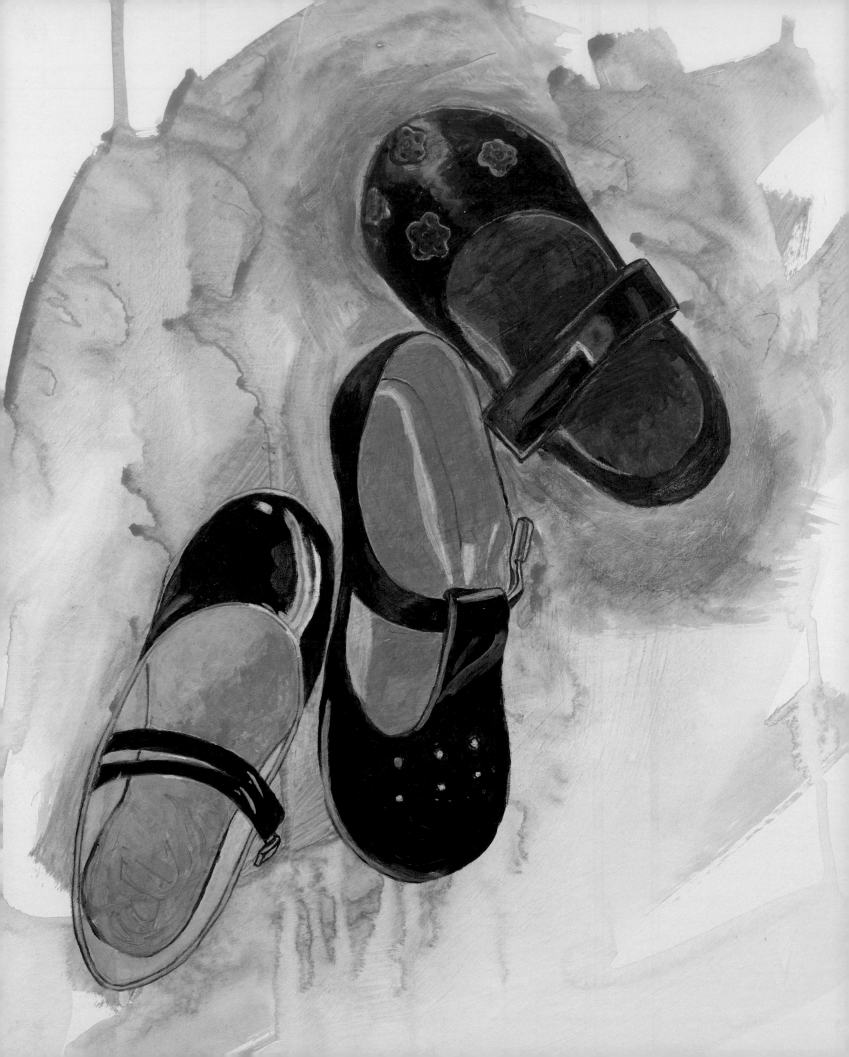

SMALL SHOES, GREAT STRIDES

How THREE BRAVE GIRLS Opened Doors to SCHOOL EQUALITY

VAUNDA MICHEAUX NELSON

illustrated by ALEX BOSTIC

Carolrhoda Books

Minneapolis

COVERED
WINDOWS

It was just the three of them and Miss Florence Meyers. Most times, only rich kids have a teacher all to themselves. Leona Tate, Tessie Prevost, and Gail Etienne were not rich. Yet, here they were. A teacher all to themselves. A classroom all to themselves. A school all to themselves. Teachers in every classroom, but no students. Just Leona, Tessie, and Gail in Miss Meyers's first-grade class.

Some people were angry about it. They surrounded the school every day, carrying signs, shouting and spitting. But Leona, Tessie, and Gail didn't hear or see much of the commotion outside. Their classroom windows were covered with brown paper, and recess was held inside. Water fountains were turned off for fear of poisoning. Strange, but this all felt normal now.

Months before, six-year-olds Leona, Tessie, and Gail couldn't have known what lay ahead when they got ready for their first day at McDonogh No. 19 Public School.

The FIRST DAY

Leona Tate's heart felt light as Mama helped her put on a sweater. Leona was glad to be leaving her crowded old school. Her dress was starched and pressed, her hair ribbon tied just right. The house was noisy with talk and filled with the delicious smells of sausage and eggs, grits and biscuits.

When a black sedan pulled up out front, the house got quiet. Two men wearing suits and yellow arm bands stepped out. One knocked on the front door. The other waited by the car, his Deputy United States Marshal badge glinting in the sun. Leona had always walked to school with Mama. Today she was getting a ride. Glory!

"When you get in the car, sit back in the seat," Leona's mother said. "Do not put your face to the window."

Mama took her hand, and they followed the marshal to the car.

Not far from Leona in the Ninth Ward, a U.S. Marshal knocked on Tessie Prevost's front door. Marshals would drive Tessie to school today too.

Mrs. Prevost told one of the lawmen, "I'm giving you my baby. This is my baby!"

"This is my job," he replied, "and I'm going to take care of this baby. You don't have to worry."

Her mother was afraid, but Tessie wasn't. The man with the badge was there, and even better, her daddy was there. Her daddy could beat Goliath and King Kong with one hand tied behind his back.

McDonogh 19 Public School was surrounded by swarms of shouting people. Leona couldn't tell what they were yelling, but it seemed to her that a parade must be coming, like a Mardi Gras morning. Leona loved the Mardi Gras celebration in New Orleans—a time for music, candy, and fun. She wondered, *Why am I going to school on a holiday?*

The road to McDonogh 19, St. Claude Avenue, was a parade route. Grandma Dora had brought Tessie there to watch celebrations many times. Like Leona, when Tessie saw the crowds of people and police on horseback, she guessed it must be Mardi Gras.

When they got to school, her daddy said, "Put your hand in my hand, and look straight ahead. Don't worry about a thing. I'm here." Tessie reached for him.

U.S. Marshals took six-year-old Gail Etienne to school that day too, but Gail could tell it wasn't a time to celebrate. Looking out of the car window, she knew right away the roaring crowd had nothing to do with Mardi Gras.

What were they so mad about? What had Gail done? Policemen held back the mob of people who seemed to want to get at her. Gail was sure they would hurt her if they could. She was glad Mama and Daddy could come along.

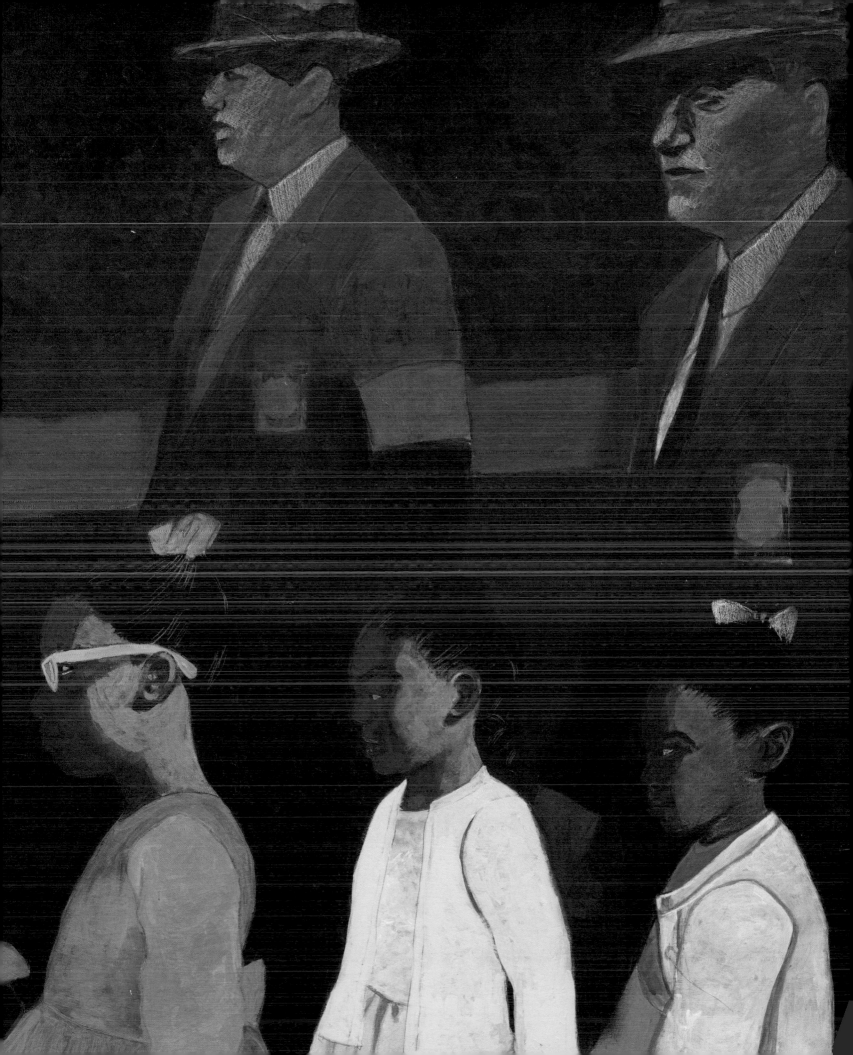

STEPPING into HISTORY

Leona held tight to Mama's hand, still unsure of what was happening on this loud and curious morning.

Tessie did as her daddy said and looked straight ahead as marshals escorted them past the screaming crowd and into McDonogh 19.

Gail climbed the stairs of the school and followed Tessie into the building. She felt tears rising but held them back with a deep breath. The federal marshal walking beside Gail gently squeezed her hand. She wouldn't cry.

As the girls entered the school, the white mob, kept across the street by police, booed. A smaller group of black supporters, being held toward the back of the school, cheered and applauded.

It was November 14, 1960, a landmark day for New Orleans and the state of Louisiana. Three little girls in ankle socks and Sunday shoes made history just by going to school.

The United States Supreme Court had ruled that it was wrong to separate students because of their skin color. School districts were ordered to integrate—to put black and white children together—and make sure *everyone* got the same education. Many districts resisted but eventually were forced to follow the law.

In New Orleans, the parents of 137 black first graders applied to have their children transferred to all-white schools. School board officials didn't want integration, so they designed an approval process requiring a series of tests most children couldn't pass. But Leona, Tessie, and Gail excelled.

At 9:15 on that historic morning, they were the first black children to enter McDonogh 19 Public School. In fact, they were the first black children to enter any previously all-white school in Louisiana since 1877 when segregation was enacted.

Ten minutes later, U.S. Marshals escorted six-year-old Ruby Bridges into the all-white William Frantz Elementary School across town. Ruby, too, had passed the tests.

CONFUSION
and
HATE

Leona, Tessie, Gail, and their parents waited on a bench in the hall near the McDonogh school office for a long time. School had started in September, so the other children were already in class. The girls squirmed and fidgeted. They played hopscotch on the tile floor to pass the time. It seemed the people in charge didn't know what to do with them.

At last the girls were taken to Miss Meyers's first-grade classroom. At last their school day could begin.

But it didn't, not yet.

Just as the girls took their seats, the white students started leaving. Their moms and dads rushed in one by one and took them out.

"Hello," Leona said to a girl sitting next to her. The girl didn't say anything. She didn't even look at Leona. Leona felt invisible. A moment later, the girl was gone.

Some of the kids wanted to stay. But their parents pulled them from their desks saying, "Come on. Let's go!"

By the end of the school day, the only children in Miss Meyers's classroom were Leona, Tessie, and Gail. It was the same the next day and the next day and the next. By the end of the week, they were the only children left in the entire school. All of the teachers at McDonogh 19 kept coming to work, but only Miss Meyers had students to teach.

Protesters continued gathering outside the school each day. They booed and shouted ugly words. They believed black children and white children should not learn together. They believed whites were better and that their children would be tainted by "mixing" with blacks.

Rowdy teenagers skipped school to be part of the angry mob. Through it all, Leona, Tessie, and Gail got up every morning and went to school.

MISS MEYERS

Like all teachers, Miss Meyers had rules.
Leona, Tessie, and Gail were not allowed
to go near the covered windows, not even
to sharpen their pencils. At recess, the girls
stayed indoors. The playground was not safe.
They brought their lunches and ate in the
classroom or under a
nearby stairwell.

Miss Meyers was kind and caring. She ate her own lunch with them, sat nearby during recess, and took them across the hall to the bathroom—all together. Like a mother keeping watch over her children, Miss Meyers never let the girls out of her sight.

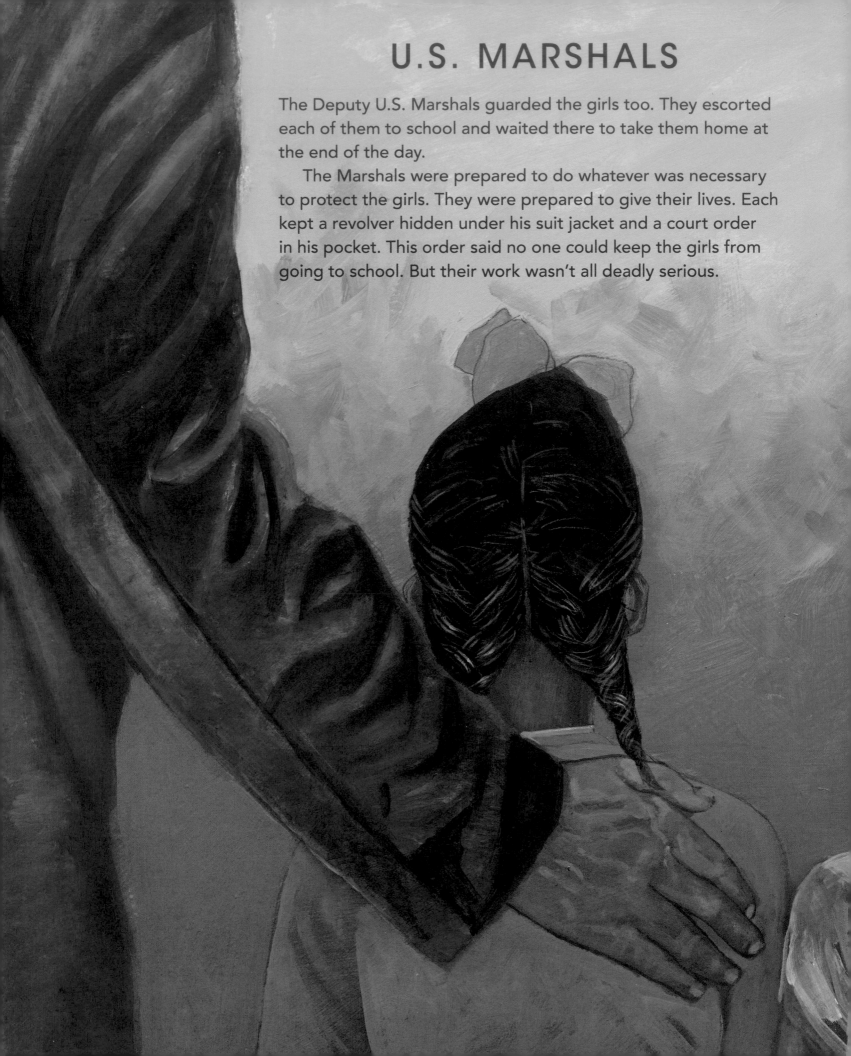

U.S. MARSHALS

The Deputy U.S. Marshals guarded the girls too. They escorted each of them to school and waited there to take them home at the end of the day.

The Marshals were prepared to do whatever was necessary to protect the girls. They were prepared to give their lives. Each kept a revolver hidden under his suit jacket and a court order in his pocket. This order said no one could keep the girls from going to school. But their work wasn't all deadly serious.

Leona was a giggler. She giggled so much that Marshal Al Butler gave her the nickname Gigglebox. When he said, "Hey, Gigglebox," she giggled even more.

Gail had a crush on Marshal Warren Emmerton. Ever since he'd squeezed her hand on that first day of school, she called him her "boyfriend." Gail beamed like sunshine when he held her hand to walk her in and out of the school each day.

"Did you have a nice day?" Marshal Herschel Garner often asked Tessie after school. "Do you have any homework?"

Tessie grinned. "Yes, sir, Mr. Herschel."

The marshals were kind, but they never lost focus on the dangerous job they were there to do—protect Leona, Tessie, and Gail.

POLICE
and
DEATH
THREATS

At night, local police sat in squad cars parked in the dark outside the girls' homes.

When a man in a black car stopped in front of Gail's house, police spotlights flashed on. Gail's daddy pushed the screen door open. Gail followed, peeking from behind him. Her eyes grew wide as police pulled a long gun from the trunk of the man's car and put him in handcuffs.

One night, some white women drove by and threw a rock at Leona's mama while she was sitting on her own porch.

And there were death threats. Someone drove a funeral hearse up and down Tessie's street every day for months. Once, Gail's father received a package containing a dead bird.

Tessie had a fenced-in yard, so she could go outside after school and play with her dog, a beagle named Mike. But Leona and Gail had to stay inside. "It's like a jail," Leona said. Her friends teased her about these rigid rules. She sometimes spent weekends with her aunt and uncle in a different part of town. Police watched over her there too.

Protesters telephoned the girls' families and threatened them. The families changed their phone numbers again and again, but somehow, people got the new ones.

"You should be ashamed!" Tessie's Grandma Dora told callers. "Does your preacher know you are doing this?"

MIXED MESSAGES

The girls received lots of mail too. Most of the messages were gladdening, some even beautiful, like songs of praise. Others were hateful. Mail was not delivered to their homes but taken to the local office of the National Association for the Advancement of Colored People (NAACP). Members of the NAACP read the letters before giving them to the girls' families. Leona, Tessie, and Gail saw only the cheerful ones. Cards and messages came from all over the world and in many languages. Some supportive folks wrote repeatedly—every week or at special holiday times like Christmas or Easter. Even former First Lady Eleanor Roosevelt sent a letter of encouragement and hope.

Meanwhile, at city hall, at school board offices, and in other parts of New Orleans, police broke up daily clashes between white and black citizens—those for or against school integration. Some people were badly hurt and had to be taken to the hospital. Hundreds were arrested, including teenagers.

SHELTER in the STORM

Despite the tempest, the girls were happy to go to school. Miss Meyers's classroom was their shelter in this storm. They ate together, played together, and learned together. Gail liked math. Leona's favorite subject was spelling. Tessie liked spelling too, but her best days were when "the piano man" came to share the magic of music.

For their entire first-grade year, the three girls remained the only students at McDonogh 19—with one exception. In January of 1961, a white family dared to send their two sons to the school. Protesters were furious. They thought all white families should take part in the boycott and keep their children out of McDonough 19. They took their signs and shouts to the home of the two boys and to where their father worked. The two attended only a few days before their family was forced to leave town. These boys were older and in different classrooms, so Leona, Tessie, and Gail never even saw them.

The girls settled in to the familiar routine of a classroom with only the three of them. It felt normal. The steady adults around them—their loving parents, attentive Miss Meyers, and the vigilant U.S. Marshals—made learning possible by keeping watch and surrounding them with calm. The girls' friendship grew strong.

UNCOVERED WINDOWS

Second grade again began with Leona, Tessie, and Gail as the only students at McDonogh 19. But after the Christmas holiday, things changed. About twenty-five new students arrived at the school. All but one were first graders, and only two were white. A single white girl joined the second-grade class.

Leona, Tessie, and Gail were excited to go outside for recess and play with other kids in the schoolyard. Protesters were mostly gone and so were the U.S. Marshals. Windows were uncovered and water fountains turned back on. The girls could eat lunch in the cafeteria. Although their teacher, Miss Inell Manning, wasn't as nice as Miss Meyers, she wasn't mean. She did her job, and Leona, Tessie, and Gail did theirs.

THE McDONOGH THREE:
Sisters for Life

Over time, they became known as the McDonogh Three. The girls formed a bond that has never broken. They grew as close as sisters and continue to stay in touch and support one another to this very day.

Leona, Tessie, Gail, and pioneers like them helped to open doors so all children could receive the education they deserve—so no one could ever again say, *You can't go to school here because of your skin color.* With all they faced, the girls and their parents didn't give up. They paved the way for white children and black children to sit side by side, learning with and from each other.

There is still work to do in schools across the nation. But Leona Tate, Tessie Prevost, and Gail Etienne—with courage and dignity—made a lasting difference.

These three unlikely leaders in small shoes took great strides for us all.

AFTER McDONOGH 19:
"House of Horror"—
Thomas J. Semmes Elementary

By law, the school district had to keep putting black and white students in the same classrooms. When it came time for Leona, Tessie, and Gail to move up to third grade, they were sent, along with black children from other schools, to Thomas J. Semmes Elementary, another previously all-white school in the Ninth Ward.

At Semmes, there were no U.S. Marshals to watch over the girls. There was no Miss Meyers. They were on their own. Here the white students didn't leave. Many didn't want an integrated school—and showed it.

They spat on the black kids and called them hurtful names. They punched them, shoved them, kicked and tripped them. A boy hit Gail in the stomach with a baseball bat. A girl ripped the front of Gail's dress. Tessie had her clothes torn too. A boy sitting behind Leona on the school bus kicked her seat until it broke. Then he spat in her hair. Leona closed her eyes. She would never forget the odor of that spit. The bus driver reported Leona for breaking the seat.

One girl was frightened when she accidentally touched Gail. Surprised, she said, "Look! My skin didn't change! I didn't turn black!"

Where did she get that crazy, silly idea, Gail thought.

The girls' third-grade teacher, Miss Anna Caruso, was like Miss Manning in second grade—neither mean nor nice, but fair. Most teachers at Semmes pretended not to see what was happening to the black students, but there were those who were outwardly cruel. One, who often brought brownies or cookies to school, gave treats to the white children but never to the black students. Another teacher held a handkerchief to her nose when black students passed, saying they smelled. Some teachers called them racist names and urged white students to be unkind, even to physically harm the black kids. "Hit her!" one teacher said.

Leona remembers Semmes Elementary as "a house of horror." Tessie calls it "the devil's domain." Learning collided with the hate and abuse they endured every day. They were afraid to eat in the cafeteria. Kids knocked their lunches out of their hands and spat in their food. The girls were afraid to use the restrooms where they could be cornered and assaulted. At recess, Leona, Tessie, Gail, and other black students huddled around a little tree in the schoolyard. They couldn't all fit around its small trunk and flimsy branches, but they found some comfort and safety in numbers.

"They don't want us there," Leona told her mother after school. Mrs. Tate hugged her and said, "Everyone is watching. You must set a good example."

Tessie didn't want to worry her parents or her Grandma Dora, so she told her troubles to her beagle, Mike. It helped, but her stomach often hurt even though she wasn't really sick.

"*Some* white kids want to play with us," Gail told her daddy, "but if anybody is watching, they won't. They sneak."

"Somebody is telling them not to play with you," her father said. "Somebody is teaching them that. You just be your best."

Leona, Tessie, and Gail were their best selves. They studied hard and bravely held their tempers. When they were mistreated, their parents wrote to school officials and filed complaints with the principal and with the NAACP. But nothing really changed for them at school. Still, Leona, Tessie, and Gail survived. They survived and helped change our nation.

MORE ABOUT SCHOOL DESEGREGATION IN NEW ORLEANS

Prior to this project, I knew only of Ruby Bridges's role in desegregating New Orleans schools. I found she wasn't the first. Leona Tate, Gail Etienne, and Tessie Prevost preceded her—by ten minutes. Leona, Tessie, Gail, and Ruby became known as the New Orleans Four.

Originally, five children were selected, but the student who was supposed to attend Frantz Elementary with Ruby was withdrawn at the last minute.

On May 17, 1954, in the *Brown v. Board of Education of Topeka, Kansas*, decision, the United States Supreme Court ruled that segregation in public schools was unconstitutional and harmful to black children. Since the court did not state a specific time requirement for desegregation, many school districts across the South, including Orleans Parish Public Schools, used the vagueness of the order to delay.

After six years of foot-dragging and finally facing a compelling order to act from Federal District Court Judge J. Skelly Wright, the Orleans Parish School Board came up with a plan to desegregate on a grade-by-grade basis starting with first grade. Black families were given only nine business days to apply in person for "transfer" of their children, and these students had to undergo a series of tests and interviews. Louisiana Governor Jimmie H. Davis and the state legislature tried to block the desegregation order. Some officials even wanted to close the schools. But Judge Wright issued a restraining order against any such actions. NAACP attorney Thurgood Marshall, who later became the first African American U.S. Supreme Court justice, also worked to make sure the court ruling was followed. He filed motions to prevent state officials from interfering. Although it was a deliberately token integration, on Monday, November 14, 1960, New Orleans Public Schools were officially desegregated.

The Orleans Parish School Board selected two schools in the Lower Ninth Ward, a racially mixed, blue-collar community. Many whites living there already felt like second-class citizens, so they saw this action as an added humiliation and protested. Influential white segregationists established a private school for whites who removed their children from McDonogh 19 and Frantz schools. But not all white citizens fought desegregation, even if they didn't agree. Some moderate whites formed Save Our Schools and the Committee on Public Schools to keep facilities open and encourage white parents to send their children to public school.

Crowds watch as white parents remove their children from McDonogh 19 Public School on November 14, 1960.

NORMAN ROCKWELL'S *THE PROBLEM WE ALL LIVE WITH*

Many people believe that Ruby Bridges is the little girl in the Norman Rockwell painting—*The Problem We All Live With*. But, according to Stephanie Plunkett, chief curator at the Norman Rockwell Museum in Stockbridge, Massachusetts, "The child pictured in *The Problem We All Live With* is not specifically Ruby Bridges but rather a symbolic child representing the racial integration of America's public schools mandated by the 1954 *Brown v. Board of Education* ruling outlawing segregation in public education. The painting was published to commemorate the tenth anniversary of that ruling."

Plunkett added, "The model was a Stockbridge, Massachusetts, girl named Lynda Jean Gunn, granddaughter of David Gunn, chairman of the Berkshire chapter of the NAACP, of which Rockwell was a member. . . . The dress that she wears was made by a local dressmaker specifically for the part, and is now in our collection."

In short, the child in Rockwell's painting represents Leona, Tessie, Gail, Ruby, and every other child who was a "first" to enter a segregated school amidst protest.

Two U.S. Marshals also served as unexpected models for the painting. According to David Turk, United States Marshals Service historian, Rockwell asked to borrow badges to pin on his models, but the badges were considered "accountable property" and legally could not be loaned. In a show of support and good humor, the service sent the badges "with deputies attached" to Rockwell's Stockbridge home studio.

The Problem We All Live With is Norman Rockwell's iconic 1964 image representing the Civil Rights Movement in the United States.

MORE ABOUT THE McDONOGH THREE

LEONA TATE

After one year at Semmes, Leona transferred to Frantz Elementary for fourth grade, then went on to integrate Joseph Kohn Junior High School and, finally, Francis T. Nicholls High School. All were part of the district's integration plan, and all were schools also attended by Ruby Bridges. In eleventh grade, Leona, Gail, Ruby, and other black students at Nicholls won a battle to change the school mascot from the Confederate flag to the bobcat.

After high school, Leona attended Parrish-Draughon Business School in San Antonio, Texas. She went on to work for South Central Bell Telephone Company, AT&T, and the United States Postal Service, all in New Orleans. In 2009, she established Leona Tate Foundation for Change, Inc., to preserve the history and role of the Lower Ninth Ward in the Civil Rights Movement and to promote racial equality through education. Leona received a Doctor of Humane Letters in 2023 from Saint Thomas Christian University in Florida.

"My mother, Louise Tate, firmly believed no door should be closed to me because of the color of my skin," Leona said. "My mom was courageous. She'd fight like a bull. . . . As a child, I realized I was doing something different; as an adult, I realized the impact.

"The primary focus was never our being able to sit next to white children in a classroom," said Leona. "We wanted current, up-to-date books and scholastic materials, quality classroom and gymnasium facilities, just like our white counterparts. It was never about 'forced integration.' It was, and still is, about fairness and equality."

Today, Leona is executive director of the Leona Tate Foundation and of the Lower Ninth Ward Living Museum, working to rebuild the community she calls home. And she didn't stop there. With the moral and fundraising support of community partners, Leona acquired the abandoned McDonogh 19 building, had it registered as a National Historic Landmark, then renovated and, in 2022, reopened the old school as the Tate Etienne Prevost (TEP) Interpretive Center. The center's mission is "to teach, exhibit and engage visitors in New Orleans Civil Rights history."

Leona takes pride in the important work she is doing but says her highest honor is her role as mother of three, grandmother of twelve, and great-grandmother of eight.

TESSIE PREVOST WILLIAMS

Tessie stayed at Semmes through the sixth grade, then told her parents she had had enough. She was through attending integrated schools. They honored their daughter's wishes and allowed her to transfer to the all-black Rivers Frederick Junior High. There Tessie found a love of school she had never known. She blossomed, especially in music, learning to play the flute and joining the school band. "Rivers Frederick was a blessing for me." Tessie said, "It changed my life." Tessie went on to graduate from the all-black Joseph S. Clark High School. She worked for twenty-seven years with the Department of Pediatric Dentistry at Louisiana State University Health Science Center in New Orleans.

"I'd like to recognize the courage and strength it took for our families. They are the heroes, really and truly. It must have been very difficult for my parents to see me come home every day beaten down emotionally, physically, and still have that encouragement to continue."

Tessie and her grandmother Dora prayed every morning and night, and not just for themselves. They prayed for her teachers, the U.S. Marshals, New Orleans—even the protesters.

"I don't think I realized the importance of what we were doing then. It wasn't until some years later," Tessie said. "I know it was worth it."

GAIL ETIENNE

Gail attended T.J. Semmes Elementary through the sixth grade, then went to Rivers Frederick Junior High with Tessie Prevost. Gail integrated Francis T. Nicholls High School with Leona Tate and Ruby Bridges. She attended Southern University and Meadows Business College. Her working career included twelve years at South Central Bell Telephone Company, eleven years at Louisiana State University Medical Center, and nearly twenty-five years with the U.S. Postal Service in New Orleans and Tulsa, Oklahoma.

"Our parents made sacrifices and went through a lot for us. It was an important thing for my dad. He was concerned about me, especially at Semmes. We really had a time at Semmes. It was rough. It was heavy on his heart. My dad wasn't a violent man, so what he would do is write letters to the school. He was steady writing those letters but, of course, nothing was done.

"Later my father said if he had to make the choice to do it again, he would do it again because it was something that needed to be done. He wanted me to have the best opportunities that I could have."

THE U.S. MARSHALS SERVICE

The United States Marshals Service is the nation's oldest federal law enforcement agency. Its motto is "Justice, Integrity, Service," and the marshals live by it.

When the Congress of the United States established the judiciary system in 1789, the first U.S. Marshals were appointed to uphold the Constitution, enforce federal laws, and ensure federal court orders were carried out. Deputy U.S. Marshals were employed to assist in these duties.

U.S. Marshals were present during many of the important events in American history. They helped keep the peace on the frontier; protected black freedmen and their families after the Civil War and during Reconstruction; enforced desegregation on southern school campuses during the Civil Rights Movement; established the Federal Witness Protection Program; arrested fugitives and illegal drug traffickers; and, during wartime, exchanged spies and prisoners of war with foreign countries. The U.S. Marshals Service, for a time (eighty years) even took the national census.

First graders Leona Tate, Gail Etienne, and Tessie Prevost escorted by (front to back) U.S. Marshals Al Butler, Warren Emmerton, and Herschel Garner at McDonogh 19 on November 14, 1960

The U.S. Marshals Service is not without controversy. Prior to the Civil War, the service was charged with enforcing Fugitive Slave Laws, which returned escaped slaves to their owners while, at the same time, U.S. Marshals inspected ships in southern waters for illegal African slave trade activities. Whether or not they agreed personally with what they were enforcing, Marshals did what they were tasked. It has been said if there's a hard job to be done, bring in the U.S. Marshals.

After Marshal Al Butler died and was cremated, his wife, Pat, returned to New Orleans to spread some of his ashes on the McDonogh 19 school grounds and to give some to Leona, Tessie, and Gail. Marshal Butler had made this request saying, "I was involved in an awful lot of things during my career. But nothing was as heartwarming and satisfying as putting those little girls in school. . . . It was not only the law. It was right." Each of the three women keeps a small container of Marshal Butler's ashes, in memory of a man who kept them safe. As Tessie recalls, even when they reunited fifty years later, "You could see the protectiveness in his face, like he was saying, 'I got this.'"

AUTHOR'S NOTE

My research for this project was wonderful and challenging. The fact that my main "characters" are still living was a new and marvelous experience for me. Leona, Tessie, and Gail, and retired Deputy U.S. Marshal Herschel Garner were kind, generous, and enthusiastic in sharing their stories and giving me their blessings on the project. I feel I've not only taken an unforgettable journey, I've made new friends, too.

Many family photos, letters (including correspondence from Eleanor Roosevelt), and other documents regarding the lives of Leona, Tessie, and Gail sadly were lost in Hurricane Katrina in 2005. Likewise, Katrina destroyed some official records of the New Orleans Public School System, so archival materials were often unavailable or incomplete. Handwritten notes by McDonogh 19 Principal John A. Stewart offered some insights into the plan for the three girls' arrival at the school but left questions unanswered. I could not determine the exact number of students who attended McDonogh 19 in the second half of the three girls' second-grade year nor the number of black students who entered T. J. Semmes with them in 1962.

I drew conclusions based on articles and recollections by Leona, Tessie, and Gail. Exploring this undertold story was enlightening and inspiring. It has been my honor.

The decision not to capitalize the words *black* and *white* in this book is my own. This reflects usage during the 1960s, the time period when these events took place. Additionally, I feel that choices about capitalization should be the prerogative of the individual writer, and I am grateful to Lerner Publishing Group for respecting my decision.

GLOSSARY

boycott: an act of protest to bring about change by refusing to interact with a person, place, or thing

desegregate: to remove legal barriers that separate people by race

evaluate: to examine and judge carefully

integrate: to remove legal and social barriers that impose segregation upon racial groups to permit free and equal association; sometimes used interchangeably with desegregation

landmark: a turning point in history

Mardi Gras: a celebration featuring parades of costumed merrymakers the day before the beginning of Lent leading up to Easter; French for "Fat Tuesday"

mixing: allowing people of different races or ethnic groups to associate

NAACP: The National Association for the Advancement of Colored People, jointly formed by blacks and whites in 1909 to advance the civil and human rights of African Americans, then known as "colored people"

protesters: individuals or groups who object to or speak strongly against or in favor of something

segregate: to separate people by race

tainted: to damage or spoil something due to contact with something considered dirty or inferior

WEBSITES FOR MORE INFORMATION

Leona Tate Foundation
www.LeonaTateFoundation.org

Tate Etienne Prevost Center
www.tepcenter.org

The United States Marshals Museum
www.usmmuseum.org

SELECTED BIBLIOGRAPHY

Books

Baker, Liva. *The Second Battle of New Orleans: The Hundred-Year Struggle to Integrate the Schools*. New York: HarperCollins Publishers, 1996.

Crain, Robert L. *The Politics of School Desegregation*. New York: Doubleday and Company, 1969.

Devlin, Rachel. *A Girl Stands at the Door: The Generation of Young Women Who Desegregated America's Schools*. New York: Basic Books, 2018.

Gerdes, Caroline. *An Oral History of the New Orleans Ninth Ward*. Gretna, LA: Pelican, 2017.

Sommer, Robin Langley. *The History of the U.S. Marshals: The Proud Story of America's Legendary Lawmen*. Philadelphia: Courage Books, 1993.

Turk, David S. (U.S. Marshals Service Historian). *Forging the Star: The Official Modern History of the United States Marshals Service*. Denton: University of North Texas Press, 2016.

Wieder, Alan. *Race and Education: Narrative Essays, Oral Histories, and Documentary Photography*. New York: Peter Lang, 1997.

Interviews and Videos

Etienne, Gail, and Leona Tate. Interview with the author at the Doubletree by Hilton Hotel, Fort Smith, AR, September 24, 2019.

Gail Etienne-Stripling Oral History. Interviewed by Mark Cave, November 18, 2017, at the Lower Ninth Ward Living Museum, New Orleans. Project: NOLA Resistance, MSS 936.

Garner, Herschel, retired U.S. Marshal. Interview with the author at the Doubletree by Hilton Hotel, Fort Smith, AR, September 23, 2019.

Leona Tate Oral History. Interviewed by Mark Cave, February 21, 2018, at the Lower Ninth Ward Living Museum, New Orleans. Project: NOLA Resistance, MSS 936.

Leona Tate Oral History. Interviewed by Mark Cave, August 13, 2012. Historic New Orleans Collection.

Tate, Leona. Interview with the author at the Lower Ninth Ward Living Museum in New Orleans, June 26, 2018.

Tate, Leona. Telephone interview with the author, March 13, 2018.

Tessie Prevost Williams Oral History. Interviewed by Mark Cave, August 3, 2017, in LaPlace, LA. Project: NOLA Resistance, MSS 936.

"Through a Crowd Bravely: 50th Anniversary of Public School Desegregation in New Orleans." Video parts I and II. New Orleans: Tulane University, November 13, 2010.

Williams, Tessie Prevost. Interview with the author at the Doubletree by Hilton Hotel, Fort Smith, AR, September 24, 2019.

Articles and Unpublished Documents

"Desegregation of Public Schools Is Carried Out without Violence: Negro Children Attend Two Integrated Schools Here." New Orleans *Times-Picayune*, November 15, 1960.

Directory of the Public Schools of New Orleans, Session 1959–1960, Session 1960–1961, Session 1961–1962. Orleans Parish School Board Collection (MSS 147). Louisiana and Special Collections, Earl K. Long Library, University of New Orleans.

Hitchens, Leslie Theresa. "The Beauty of Hatred: The McDonogh Three's Untold Stories" (2015). Hamline University: School of Education Student Capstone Theses and Dissertations.

Juniper, Clare. "It Was Worth It." *Southern Exposure* 7, no. 57 (Summer 1979): 60–61.

Louisiana State Advisory Committee. *The New Orleans School Crisis: Report of the Louisiana State Advisory Committee to the United States Commission on Civil Rights*. Washington, DC: U.S. Government Printing Office, 1961.

"McDonogh 19 Elementary School." National Register of Historic Places. National Park Service, U.S. Department of Interior, August 12, 2016.

School Board Bound Minutes, vol. 41, 1960–1961. Orleans Parish School Board Collection (MSS 147). Series: Louisiana and Special Collections, Earl K. Long Library, University of New Orleans.

Steward, John. Personal and faculty notes of McDonogh 19 Elementary School principal, November 11, 14, and 15, 1960. Amistad Research Center, Tulane University.

Tate, Leona. "Gliding Past Mobs, Toward an Education." New Orleans *Times-Picayune*, May 20, 2004.

Thevenot, Brian. "The McDonogh Three: *Brown vs. Board of Education* 1954, School Integration 50 Years Later." New Orleans *Times-Picayune*, May 16, 2004.

> "I lived three blocks from McDonogh 19. I was in the district. Why shouldn't I be able to go there?"
> —TESSIE

> "A lot of people made a lot of sacrifices for us to get to that point . . . that day . . . that time."
> —GAIL

Escorted by Deputy U.S. Marshals, Leona, Tessie, and Gail enter McDonogh 19 Public School.

New Orleans police officers hold back hundreds of people observing Leona, Tessie, and Gail as they are escorted home by U.S. Marshals after their first day at McDonogh 19 Public School. New Orleans police were practiced in controlling crowds because of expertise gained during Mardi Gras.

> "Born in 1954, the same year as *Brown v. Board of Education*, we were the chosen ones."
> —LEONA

> "These were some brave girls."
> —DEPUTY U.S. MARSHAL HERSCHEL GARNER

Leona Tate, Gail Etienne, and Tessie Prevost (*left to right, back row*) stand at the entrance of McDonogh 19 Public School, the same doors they entered during integration in 1960. They are joined by Daisy Barrow, Brooklyn Charles, and Élan Jolie Hébert (*left to right, front row*) for the sixty-first anniversary ceremony on November 14, 2021.

For the brave pioneers Leona, Tessie, and Gail, their loving parents, and the courageous marshals who kept the girls safe —V.M.N.

To my good friends, Judy Harris Middleton and Linda Hampton, who were angels and guardians of my work and getting whatever I needed to get this book done —A.B.

Acknowledgments

My heart is filled with gratitude for Leona Tate, Tessie Prevost, and Gail Etienne for entrusting me with their stories, sharing so much of themselves, and blessing me with their friendship. Special thanks to Tessie's sister Tory Prevost and retired U.S. Marshal Herschel Garner for their kind contributions. I am especially grateful to Jim Dunn, president emeritus, United States Marshals Museum Foundation, for bringing this story to my attention; for introducing me to Leona, Tessie, and Gail; and for his encouragement, support, and friendship. And to everyone at the foundation and the U.S. Marshals Service. Thanks to my agent Tracey Adams, my editor Carol Hinz, art director Danielle Carnito, photo editor manager Cynthia Zemlicka, publisher Adam Lerner, and my publishing family at Lerner. And to illustrator Alex Bostic. For research assistance, I'm obliged to Phillip Cunningham, Christopher Harter, and Lee Facincani at Tulane University's Amistad Research Center; James Hodges and Ronald Joullian at the University of New Orleans Earl K. Long Special Collections Library; Norman Rockwell Museum Chief Curator Stephanie Plunkett; Curator/Historian Eric Seiferth, Senior Reference Associate Mary Lou Eichhorn, and Curator of Manuscripts Aimee Everrett at the Historic New Orleans Collection, Williams Research Center; Director of Photography David Grunfeld at The Times-Picayune/The Advocate; Rio Rancho Interlibrary loan librarians Nancy Oberdick, Joseph McKinley, and Colette Martinez; U.S. Marshals Service Historian David Turk; researcher Sarah Watson; and Christine and Amber Porter. A special embrace goes to my writing critique group—Katherine Hauth, Stephanie Farrow, Uma Krishnaswami, Caroline Starr Rose, and the late Mark Karlins. I am most beholding to my darling husband, Drew, my top editor and my best friend. Above all, I thank my Lord for enabling me to continue this fulfilling work.

Carolrhoda Books®
An imprint of Lerner Publishing Group, Inc.
241 First Avenue North
Minneapolis, MN 55401 USA

For reading levels and more information, look up this title at www.lernerbooks.com.

Photo acknowledgments: © Globe Photos/ZUMAPRESS.com via Alamy, p. 34; *The Problem We All Live With*, Norman Rockwell, 1964. Artwork Approved by the Norman Rockwell Family Agency, p. 35; Peter Forest/Getty Images, pp. 36 (top, third from top), 37 (top); Don Cravens/Getty Images, p. 36 (second from top, bottom); Times-Picayune Newspaper, p. 37 (second from top); Bettmann/Getty Images, pp. 37 (bottom), 40 (top left); AP Photo, p. 40 (top right); AP Photo/Ted Jackson, p. 40 (bottom). Design elements: Ivan Gromov/Unsplash; Aripai Leangphet/Shutterstock. Back cover photo: Times-Picayune Newspaper.

Photographs of paintings by Kamau Bostic.
Designed by Danielle Carnito.
Main body text set in Avenir LT Pro.
Typeface provided by Linotype AG.
The illustrations in this book were created with acrylic on illustration board.

Library of Congress Cataloging-in-Publication Data

Names: Nelson, Vaunda Micheaux, author. | Bostic, Alex, illustrator.
Title: Small shoes, great strides : how three brave girls opened doors to school equality / Vaunda Micheaux Nelson ; illustrated by Alex Bostic.
Description: Minneapolis, MN : Carolrhoda Books, [2023] | Includes bibliographical references. | Audience: Ages 7–11 years | Audience: Grades 4–6 | Summary: "A powerful true story about three black girls who courageously integrated a New Orleans school on November 14, 1960, told by award-winning author Vaunda Micheaux Nelson" —Provided by publisher.
Identifiers: LCCN 2022056332 (print) | LCCN 2022056333 (ebook) | ISBN 9781728419237 (Library Binding) | ISBN 9781728494104 (eBook)
Subjects: LCSH: School integration—Louisiana—New Orleans—History—20th century—Juvenile literature. | African Americans—Education—Louisiana—New Orleans—History—20th century—Juvenile literature. | Civil rights movements—Louisiana—New Orleans—History—20th century—Juvenile literature.
Classification: LCC LC214.23.N46 N45 2023 (print) | LCC LC214.23.N46 (ebook) | DDC 379.2/630976335—dc23/eng/20230113

LC record available at https://lccn.loc.gov/2022056332
LC ebook record available at https://lccn.loc.gov/2022056333

Manufactured in the United States of America
1-49038-49255-5/2/2023